ORCHARD BOOKS
338 Euston Road, London, NW1 3BH
Orchard Books Australia
Level 17/207, Kent Street, Sydney, NSW 2000

First published in hardback in Great Britain in 2009
First paperback publication in 2010

Text © Cressida Cowell 2009
Illustrations © Neal Layton 2009

The rights of Cressida Cowell to be identified as the author
and of Neal Layton to be identified as the illustrator of this
work has been asserted by them in accordance with the
Copyright, Designs and Patents Act, 1988.

A CIP catalogue record of this book
is available from the British Library.

ISBN 978 1 40830 203 3

5 7 9 10 8 6 4

Printed in China

Designed by David Mackintosh

Orchard Books is a division of
Hachette Children's Books,
an Hachette UK Company

www.hachette.co.uk

FOR ELEY the Elephant.
N.L.

TO
DEAREST Simon,
who is the
want in
E...

EMILY BROWN

and the

Elephant Emergency

written by Cressida Cowell

illustrated by Neal Layton

ORCHARD

Once upon a time,
there was a little girl called Emily Brown
and an old grey rabbit called Stanley.

One day, Emily Brown and Stanley were whitewater rafting down the turbulent waters of the Zambezi River with their great friend Matilda.

Matilda was just steering them skilfully over the very last rapid with her trunk when there was a . . .

Ri-i-i-inG!

Ri-i-i-inG!

Ri-i-i-inG!

Ri-i-i-inG!

on the
emergency
telephone.

EMERGENCY
TELEPHONE

ON/OFF RING

Emily Brown answered it. "Emily Brown speaking. Can I help you?"

"Elephants don't wear wellingtons, Matilda's mummy," replied Emily Brown. "And this phone is for emergency calls only. Please do not phone unless you have an emergency."

And Emily Brown put down the phone politely.

A few days later, Emily Brown and Stanley were searching for new species in the land of the dinosaurs. They were just investigating a particularly interesting set of footprints with their good friend Matilda when there was a . . .

Ri-i-i-ing!

Ri-i-i-inG!

Ri-i-i-ing!

Ri-i-i-ing!

Ri-i-i-ing!

Ri-i-i-ing!

Ri-i-i-ing!

Ri-i-i-ing!

on the emergency telephone.

Emily Brown answered it again.
"Hello, this is Emily Brown. What is your emergency?"

"IT'S MATILDA'S MUMMY AGAIN,"
(said Matilda's mummy). "Can I speak to Matilda? I'm EVEN MORE WORRIED than I was before. I'm worried that a BRONTOSAURUS might sit on someone. I'm worried that the T. Rex might give Matilda a nip with his POINTY TEETH. And it is way past five o' clock, and Matilda hasn't had her tea yet. Matilda HAS TO HAVE HER TEA on the dot of five o' clock."

"Elephants do not have tea times, Matilda's mummy," replied Emily Brown. "Matilda will eat when she is hungry. Again, Matilda's mummy, can I ask you not to call this phone unless you have a real emergency? This telephone is for emergency calls only."

And Emily Brown put down the phone, a bit more firmly this time.

A few days later, and Emily Brown and Stanley were climbing the peak of Mount Everest. Poor Matilda was having a little trouble holding onto the rope because of her wellingtons, and her lunchbox getting in the way, there was a . . .

Ri-i-i-ing! Ri-i-i-ing!
Ri-i-i-i-ng!
Ri-i-i-i-ng!!!

Emergency telephone

on the emergency telephone

"Hello?" snapped Emily Brown. "Emily Brown speaking, and this better be a proper emergency!"

"IT CERTAINLY IS." (said Matilda's mummy).

"This is Matilda's mummy here, and I am MORE WORRIED THAN EVER.

I'm worried that Matilda might get CAUGHT IN AN AVALANCHE.

I'm worried that Matilda might get FROSTBITE ON HER TRUNK.

And Matilda seems to have forgotten to wear her NICE CLEAN SOCKS again ... Matilda is a very smart elephant and she likes to look spotless

AT ALL TIMES..."

"Matilda's mummy!" cried Emily Brown, VERY FIRMLY INDEED.
"Elephants do not wear socks, clean or otherwise!
And clean socks are not an emergency!"

A few days later still, and Emily Brown and Stanley were
searching for diamonds in the deepest-most caves of the earth . . .

but Matilda was not joining in.

She was worried
she might lose a wellington . . .

or drop her lunchbox . . .

or dirty her nice
clean socks.

So she sat and

watched Emily Brown

and Stanley

and waited for

the emergency telephone to ring. She already had her helmet on, because she knew that was what her mummy would want.

Poor Matilda waited . . .

and she
waited . . .

and she
waited . . .

by the
emergency
telephone.

But still
Matilda's
mummy did
not call.

And then poor Matilda
grew sad and ill.

Tears rolled down her
floppy trunk.

"My mummy
has forgotten
me!" cried
Matilda.

And the light on her
helmet flickered and
went out.

Emily Brown looked at Stanley.

And Stanley looked at Emily Brown.

Matilda was one unwell elephant.

THIS really *was* an
EMERGENCY.

Emily Brown picked up the emergency telephone,
and called Matilda's mummy.

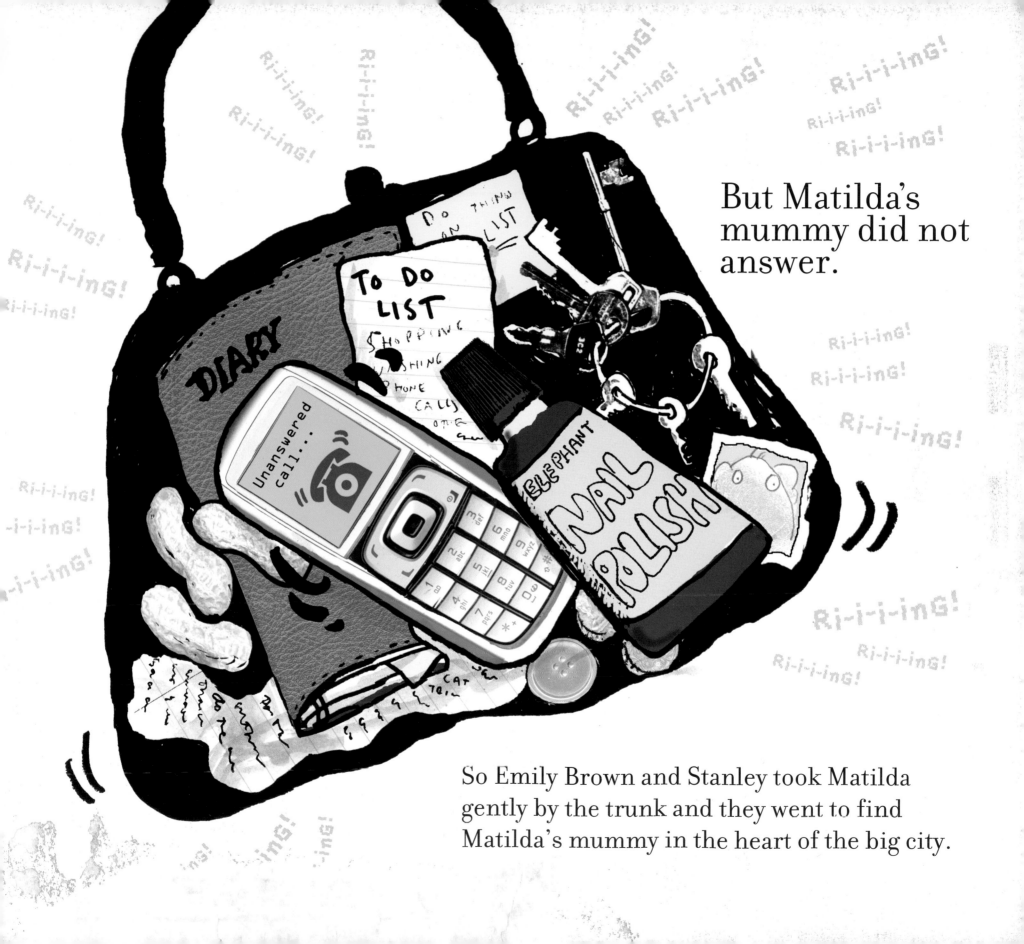

But Matilda's mummy did not answer.

So Emily Brown and Stanley took Matilda gently by the trunk and they went to find Matilda's mummy in the heart of the big city.

It turned out that Matilda's mummy needed rescuing *herself!*
She had been kidnapped by a great, grey busy–ness,
and it would not let her go.

Matilda perked up immediately.
She threw off her wellingtons,
chucked away her lunchbox,
and tossed her
clean socks into
the nearest
puddle.

IT WAS A VERY
DARING RESCUE

A few days later, Emily Brown, Stanley,
Matilda and Matilda's mummy were searching for the source of the
Nile in the jungles of Africa. They were surrounded by crocodiles,
nobody had on their wellingtons, it was way past tea time,
and Matilda's mummy's socks would have been the dirtiest of all,
if she had been wearing socks, which she wasn't.

Because elephants don't wear socks.

Suddenly there was a . . .

Ri-i-i-inG! Ri-i-i-inG!
Ri-i-i-inG!
Ri-i-i-inG!

on Matilda's mummy's mobile phone.

But one of the crocodiles ATE it.

So we'll never know what the emergency was.

I wonder if it was important?